Poems

From a

Mountain

Craig M. Lanyon

Poems

From a

Mountain

The Journey of Love

One may spend many years
Pondering what's to come
But if one ponders for too long
Then what's to come is done
So as my eyes start to see
And my soul begins to grow
I am slowly learning
I cannot harvest
The crops I do not sow
If it is love that I desire
A love that's full and true
I may have to travel many lands
Scary fun and new
I may get hurt I may get lost
I may get quite repentful
just so long as I am sailing strong
And live to my potential
So whichever way the win may blow
North south east or west
So long as I'm sailing strong
And know I've done my best
and if that day eventuates
That I find that land of love
Everyone will know
For everywhere that I shall be
So, will a golden glow
I'll be bathing in a rainbow

I'll be riding on a cloud
For of my love all will see
Of my love I'll be so proud
Yet until that day eventuates
I'll keep sailing those single man's seas
Looking for that land of love
For there I will find the keys
The keys to the chest of life
The pirates unmarked treasurer
the only jewel that we all want
A love that last forever

The Great Reef

At first glance it rippled water
With a soft light touch of blue
But on closer examination
The tales you here are true
The clean water you see from above is irresistible for a swim
Just prepare yourself for a pleasant shock
A feeling of euphoria when you jump in
Clown fish entertain for hours
They are quite aptly named
Parrot fish like their land name sakes
Are beautifully untamed
The coral that from the surface
Remains hidden from view
Burst alive with rainbow colours
As if only just for you
When each invisible current passes
It makes the ocean dance
Your listening to silent music
Full of wonder and romance
The wildlife is teaming
So alien from what's on land
Yet if you imagine being part of it
There's no feeling quite as grand
The turtles with their hard exterior
Inside are soft and scared
Not unlike many man
Who want love but never dared
The reef is another planet
In which I can never stay

I'm just blessed that I was part of it
If only for one day

Healing

With the sun setting
Some see the day as ending
Whilst others observe the dawn
Of nature's time for mending
Time to address our wounds
That were gathered in the day
To be strengthen by the positives
And to throw the rest away
But some wounds we get are deep
And without any warning
Which not even mother nature
Can expect to heal by morning
So time is the temperamental friend
As a healer it's unsurpassed
But don't turn your back on it
Or it will hurt you just as fast

Respect

We are wise at any age
Just some are wise beyond their years
These are the respected ones
By their older and wiser peers
The wise man is a listener
The wise man hears his peers
The wise man shares laughter
The wise man sheds tears
The wise man can symphathise
With souls that are indifferent
The wise man is humble
During his years of learning spent
The wise man is learned
But this he won't proclaim
For the souls that learn from him
Are wise just the same

Global Peace

Overlooking a valley of green to a distant city tempest
I realise just how dangerous the human kind can be
To every living soul
From the land and too the sea
And how ironic it does seem
That we are called the human kind
For kind isn't quite the word
That enters in my mind
We are slowly changing
The way we see the world
But it's a global effort needed
For a united flag to be unfurled
We need to change the way we think
Towards our fellow man and creature
Put aside our egos and selfish goals
To help all of mother nature
That just doesn't mean animals or trees in need of care
It also requires compassion for all humans everywhere
We are all of the same god
Like the seasons spring to fall
Just remember that love is the only thing
That is desired by all
So, if you love each day you live
And live each day you love
Then you have played your important part
In the eyes of the dove

Finding Wisdom

During our journey of life
We go through many chapters
Some we will embrace
Others will seem detractors
The life we live presently
Could be different from that envisioned
As the person that is living it
May have previously been imprisoned
Like earths vast array of animals
From small fish to eagles souring
So too are our inner selves
Just there for the exploring
we shouldn't be scared of who are
or of who we want to be
nor should we of the paths to take
to make it reality
face the world with joy and courage
and a heart that's always true
with your ever-expanding past
to teach and guide you through
cherish all experiences
with hope and awareness
to have a life of fulfilment
take risks but be not careless
mistakes are bound to happen
for how else are we to learn
the best victories in life
are the ones we truly earn

Family

My family is a tree
And I am its fruit
I am a product from its leaves
To the tip of its root
If I were to be sour
the tree would have poor seeds
yet I am blessed in that
from love my tree feeds
there may come a day
that I find fertile ground
somewhere far away
or on ground that's just around
and I may start to grow
my own tree from rare breed
and eventually I pray
my tree grows like a weed
into a forest of trees
that breaths love into the air
helping the world to live
with hope amidst despair
but I am still a fruit and over time will ripen
to continue this new forest
of which evil it will syphon
let's grow a world of happiness
where love is in its place
let's put a universal smile
on our planets face

Love and Company

Oh, how mysterious the force that blows
The wind through the sturdy trees
The same force that lets small flowers dance
On a hill in a gentle breeze
And what wonder I do have for the rising sun
To which the birds sing its praise
It's the same beauty I see in your eyes
That warms my winter days
Your name is enough alone
To send my heart to skip a beat
Yet the power you have over me
Is a challenge I must meet
What is it I need to do
To open your eyes as to who I am
Do I need to go away?
And come back a different man
But I don't want to change
Neither myself or dearest you
I just need you to know
That these words I feel are true
And if it comes to past
That your heart and mine aren't one
Then all the tears I've already shed
Are nothing for what's to come
So please look into your heart
And tell me what you see
I just pray that it's what I need
Your love and company

Confusion

If only I could see
The workings of the female mind
Maybe I would understand life
And its laws would be defined
For at the moment I am lost
In a cloud of poor judgement
And the only way I'll be found
Is by something heaven sent
I do not understand
The way that women work
I'll have a life of sadness
If it requires a merc
All I need is a woman
Who's values I do share
Someone with compassion
Someone who'll let me care
Someone with a jest for life
And forgiveness to others
Someone that sees here foes
Not as enemies but brothers
A lady that will cherish life
And smile with each day
A special person that sees the bad
In a loving way
So, if I find a replica
Of the values that I hold
I wouldn't let her go
Not for all of the world's gold

A lady like that is priceless
But that is my desire
She'd be my eternal fuel
To our everlasting fire
And I would be her air
To which we both will breath
Heaven will be our home
When this earth we do leave
Oh, powers of be
Please hear my pleading cry
For if it is not for me
Then I am fir to die
I have done all I want to do
On this world alone
So, if that's how I am to stay
Then I'm ready for home
But I do feel I will receive
The wish what I command
I just don't know when it is
Or on what land
So, I'll sit and wait patiently
For the days and nights to follow
Until I am delivered a princess
To free me from my sorrow

Mother

to my beloved Mother
you are gods reason for creating humans
you share love, compassion, kindness, forgiveness
accept who we are even with our sins all without the need for
gratitude
you help make the world sing joyful hymns
I love you as does every soul you touch
keep smiling ,onwards and upwards

Guess what? ILOVE YOU

Diary

Well it's been a long time my friend
Since I put pen to paper
Please don't feel I've forgotten you
I hope I'm not out of favour
I'm still well and in good health
Hopefully so too are the pages
I have found my love of life
May it last for ages
It was daunting at first to have the
courage to commit
And this is my ode to her
That all men should admit
Although we're strong
Although we're sometimes weak
Although we're sometimes wright
Sometimes we will feel meek
If I don't have her
And she doesn't have you
If we're both alone
What would both do

Guidance

My grandfather said to me
This farming life is not a life of glee
Leave the land of prosperity
Travel the sea and the city for me
I did what a grandson should do
Respected his advice and followed it through
I saw the sea and cited the city
I did it tough the nitty and gritty
But the driving force in the back of my mind
Is what grandfather wanted me to find
I am a man of the land
No matter how far you take me
I loved the rain in England
It was the drought breaking rain to see
I loved the dry Sahara
And the waterfalls I've been shown
Yet it didn't have the billabongs
This swagman dreamt of back home

Life and Love

Love has so many faces
But I'm trying to remember one
I feel love in the sight of morn
And when I see the rising sun
There is love in a searching bee
That lands softly on a rose
Also, in a grandparent's eyes
wiping a grandchild's nose
love is everywhere I look
if I take time to spend
it's everywhere and anywhere
but it's not my external friend
I have it inside my heart most times
Yet it's not being allowed to share
When I try to give it to someone
It gets left out in the open air
And it takes a bit of energy
To keep the giving going on
So, I try to remember faces
Of love and what's to come

Lost

I think I'm doing it again
Chasing my tail in my own back yard
I'm not sure it's what I need
I probably will fall again quite hard
It's not easy to show a smile
when you don't have a true close friend
its even harder when you think you did
but "no its not me" is the vibe they send
I might just have a quiet night
It's not bad to have some self-time
Tomorrow I might have a few drinks
The day after that is all mine
Will I keep on my road ahead?
And be picked up by a passer by
Or should I retrain the thoughts I think
To fix the problems that currently lie
I can't be that hard to understand
It maybe I'm too easy to see
But what's the point of hiding one's self
It all makes little sense to me

Belief

I never seem to trust myself
In making important decisions
But for a change I believe in me
And these are my reasons
I can see your inner beauty
Your inner strength, your soul
I can visualise life with you beside me
No matter how many years may roll
I can focus on a stable life
With you by my side
I can foresee the brighter future
I no longer need to hide
You're my rock, my base, my life long search
In war you are my soldier
And I will be with you side by side
If you need to cry, I am your shoulder
why? Because I love you